AS TEACHING G S

Pocketbook

By Dot Constable

Cartoons:
Phil Hailstone

Published by:

Teachers' Pocketbooks
Laurel House, Station Approach,
Alresford, Hampshire SO24 9JH, UK
Tel: +44 (0)1962 735573
Fax: +44 (0)1962 733637
E-mail: sales@teacherspocketbooks.co.uk
Website: www.teacherspocketbooks.co.uk

*Teachers' Pocketbooks is an imprint of
Management Pocketbooks Ltd.*

With thanks to Brin Best for his help in
launching the series.

This edition published 2005.
Reprinted 2007, 2008, 2010.

ISBN 978 1 903776 67 4

British Library Cataloguing-in-Publication
Data – A catalogue record for this book is
available from the British Library.

Design, typesetting and graphics by Efex Ltd.
Printed in UK.

Contents

Introduction

Think about walking into a classroom. You picture the children and their teacher. But take a closer look and somewhere in the room you will spot the teaching assistant (TA). Unobtrusive, smiling, taking life in their stride as they offer support to both pupils and teacher – THAT'S YOU! What would schools do without you?

They would be the first to admit that without their trusted band of teaching assistants it would be extremely difficult to function successfully. Children need help in so many ways and teachers do not always have time to deal with the many issues that arise in a school day.

In addition, the reforms of recent years have significantly increased the workload of schools and their teachers. The school improvement agenda, developments in the fields of special educational needs, inclusion, the workforce agreement and Every Child Matters (to name a few) have highlighted the need for schools to employ a range of support personnel. Schools need, more than ever before, to create and promote professional teams of teachers and TAs who can work together.

Introduction

TAs who have worked in both primary and secondary schools say the experiences are quite different. The size of schools, their ethos and management can vary considerably and because every school is different, every TA's job is different. However, there are some attributes that any school will look for in a TA:

- Patience
- Understanding
- Sense of humour
- Kindness
- Support

- Sensitivity
- Willingness
- Adaptability
- Versatility
- Diplomacy

And, wherever you work, there will be **core principles, values, procedures and practice** that every member of the school community should understand and value. One of the things this book will do is to provide you with a quick guide to what these might be.

Introduction

If you are new to the TA role, reading this book in full will help you gain an overall picture; those with experience might prefer to use it as a resource to dip into for information, ideas and strategies.

Whether you come to this book with experience or as a novice, a key point to remember is that where teachers and TAs plan and work together they will almost always be successful in providing for their pupils' needs. Use this book to enable that to happen:

- Look at roles and responsibilities
- Consider the range of support mechanisms on offer
- Evaluate your practice
- Decide what changes may need to be made
- Make those changes

If you can do this, you will most certainly be a valued and respected TA.

The Role of the TA

 Assisting the Teacher

 Assisting Pupils

 Assisting the School

 The Profession

The Role of the TA

Your place within the structure

Teaching assistants play a crucial role in enabling schools to meet the needs of their customers, the pupils. The pyramid below highlights a generic line management common in schools. At the apex is the headteacher, who has responsibility for the whole school. Levels of responsibility decrease as you work down the structure.

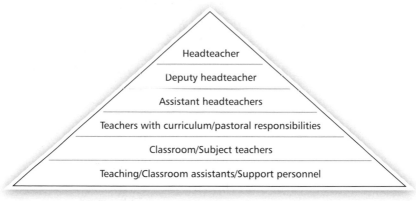

Headteacher

Deputy headteacher

Assistant headteachers

Teachers with curriculum/pastoral responsibilities

Classroom/Subject teachers

Teaching/Classroom assistants/Support personnel

Your place within the structure

As the pyramid stands, the teaching assistant has the least responsibility, but this in no way diminishes the role or importance of the TA within the structure.

Every pyramid needs a strong base to stand firm.

YOU ARE YOUR SCHOOL'S STRONG BASE!

Starting out

I met with Anna a few weeks into her new job as a teaching assistant. She told me she was totally overwhelmed by the number of things she was expected to know, to deal with and to manage. She was desperately trying to get to know all the school's routines, rules and regulations but was finding it difficult.

'I am trying really hard but they have to remember I've only just started working here and there is a lot to learn. I feel really inadequate and I'm wondering whether I'm up to the job.'

I assured Anna that she was 'up to the job' and that her worries were common amongst new members of staff in schools. Getting used to working in any school environment is no easy task – not even for teachers.

DON'T WORRY; it takes time. No one will expect you to know everything straight away – they didn't!

The value of induction

Anna's first weeks would have been so much easier if her school had provided induction. An effective induction package is valuable to both the TA and the school.

Teaching assistants who are made to feel welcome in their new job, given support settling in and given a feeling of worth will settle more quickly and confidently into the role. For schools wishing to establish and maintain a well-ordered, successful learning environment, this is essential. Good preparation on their part means their new TAs work more efficiently and effectively.

They really make me feel my work is important.

This is a really friendly school. I've settled in much quicker than I expected.

Everybody is so helpful and supportive.

What should I expect?

Whether you are starting out or transferring to a new job, you need access to and full understanding of a range of information. The following diagram is a guide to what to look for from your school induction process. It may also be a useful checklist for those of you already well established in your schools.

Information on the school:	School policies and practice:	Introduction to identified staff:

• Map of the school
• School timetable/timings
• School calendar
• Staff list
	• School handbook – make sure this includes:
	  - SEN policy
	  - Safeguarding & child protection policies
	  - Rewards systems
	  - Behaviour policy
		• Headteacher
		• Special educational needs co-ordinator (SENCO)
		• Pastoral manager(s)
		• Child protection & safeguarding officer
		• Secretary (get to know the secretary first – he/she is at the hub of what happens in a school and will be able to answer many questions)

Information relating to carrying out the work:
• Work schedule/timetable
• Access to photocopier, computer resources, equipment

WHAT I NEED TO KNOW

The following pages cover these in more detail.

Information on the school

How to find your way around the school building
A map of the school is essential. Even so, it's helpful if someone can walk you around, pointing out good routes and highlighting areas of particular importance.

The important times of the school day and year
You should be issued with a **school timetable** that not only indicates start and end of lessons/sessions but also tells you where you will be and with whom. You'll also need a **school calendar** to find out about important events and dates in the school year, eg tests/examinations, start and end of term, etc.

Who's who?
A staff list will provide you with information on who's who and what their responsibilities are. This will help you to familiarise yourself with staff names and to identify those people who may be able to answer your queries.

Key staff

Aim to meet the following as soon as you can. They are crucial to the effective running of any school.

- **The headteacher**
  You will probably have met the head at your interview, but if you didn't and you aren't welcomed by him or her on the first day, ask for an introduction. It is really important that you at least meet the 'captain of the ship' and probably more important that they meet and are able to recognise you

- **The special educational needs co-ordinator (SENCO)**
  The person responsible for special educational needs in a school is the SENCO. This person will take charge of the day-to-day organisation of special educational needs (SEN) provision throughout the school. This will include the deployment of TAs and provision of information relating to how the children's needs are to be met. You may well find the SENCO is your line manager and the person who manages your work schedule

Key staff

- **Pastoral manager(s)**
  Pastoral managers in a school have the role of overseeing the welfare and care of pupils. They deal with a whole range of issues including: attendance, pupils who need emotional support, cases of bullying, pupils with poor/inappropriate behaviour. This role may be undertaken by a deputy headteacher/assistant headteacher/heads of year, depending on the type and size of the school

- **Child protection & safeguarding officer (CPSO)**
  Every school has to have a child protection & safeguarding officer. This will be a senior member of the school staff. If you are not given information on child protection & safeguarding, ask to meet with the CPSO to discuss it

- **School secretary/admin staff**
  The school secretary is possibly the most helpful person you will encounter in the school, particularly while you settle in. He/she will be able to answer a lot of your basic queries about the general running of the school and will almost certainly be able to direct you to who you might need to see regarding particular issues

Carrying out your work

It will probably be your line manager who provides you with your timetable and instructions on the work to be carried out. You will need:

- A personal timetable that identifies teachers, classes and rooms so you know who you are with, where and at what times

- Information about your roles and responsibilities for carrying out your work within that set timetable

- Information about where and how to access relevant resources/equipment

- A method of feeding back so that there are opportunities for you to talk to your line manager about your work – both the successful elements and any that are creating difficulties for you. Problems can only be sorted out if they are talked about. **Don't be afraid to discuss them**

School policies and practice

Every school must have regard to the five outcomes set out in the *Every Child Matters: Change for Children in Schools* (DfES 2004e) document that requires them to ensure children:

- Are healthy
- Stay safe
- Enjoy and achieve
- Make a positive contribution
- Achieve economic and social well-being

To provide for this, schools as communities require working practices that ensure all who are involved in them are able to work in harmony to achieve the outcomes.

In light of this, as a teaching assistant, the policies you should be very aware of are:

1. Safeguarding and child protection
2. Special educational needs (SEN)
3. Behaviour management

They are central to your role in the school, and having a sound understanding of their associated procedures is vital.

Child protection policy

All staff working with children should be able to recognise suspected signs of child abuse and subsequently know what action to take. The school's child protection policy should set down information relating to this and outline procedures for action to be taken when there is cause for concern.

As a TA you need to be aware of the types of abuse that children may encounter:

Emotional – where, for example, there is lack of love, or verbal abuse
Physical – where the child is physically harmed
Sexual – where the child is exploited sexually
Neglect – where the child's basic needs are not being met

Signs of abuse could be marks/bruising on the child; comments made by the child, other children or adults; observations made by adults on children's changing patterns of behaviour. If you have the slightest suspicion that a child is in distress and possibly being abused you **must** report it to the school's child protection officer.

Child protection policy

The child protection policy

Should provide details of the school's responsibility as defined in the 1989 Children Act to have a 'duty of care' to its children. The act states:

'The welfare of the child shall be the paramount consideration.'

Staff have a responsibility to be aware of the policy, the needs of its children and in turn to respond to need.

If a child wishes to discuss particular issues with you, **you must not guarantee confidentiality.**

If you are concerned about the welfare of a child, report it to the identified child protection officer. **You must not question the child.**

As a general principle, you should not make unnecessary physical contact with pupils. There may well be times, however, when you need to comfort a child who is upset. **Make sure this is done in an open/overt way.**

All staff working with children in schools have to receive training on child protection and this must be updated every three years

SEN Policy

A central part of your role as TA may well be to support pupils who have special educational needs (SEN) and, therefore, you will need to be familiar with the school's SEN policy.

The SEN Code of Practice 2001 states that all schools **must** have an SEN policy and it **must** contain information on:

- The school's provision for special educational needs
- The identification, assessment and associated provision for all pupils with SEN
- Staffing and partnerships with bodies beyond the school

The person responsible for the policy is the special educational needs coordinator (SENCO) who, in line with the policy, will take responsibility for the day-to-day organisation of SEN provision throughout the school. This will include the deployment of TAs and provision of information relating to how the children's needs are to be met.

SEN Policy

You will need to familiarise yourself with the SEN Code of Practice and the SEN policy but as a start, initial important factors to note are:

> Pupils who have been identified as having special educational needs will be supported at one of three identified levels of intervention called: SCHOOL ACTION
> SCHOOL ACTION PLUS or
> STATEMENT OF SPECIAL EDUCATIONAL NEED.

> To facilitate the support and to enable pupils to progress, those with identified special educational needs will have an individual education plan (IEP) outlining their needs, their targets for improvement and information on how the school intends to provide for meeting those needs and targets (including use of TA support).

> Pupil reviews will take place to ascertain progress made. **For those pupils who have a written statement of SEN, an annual review of progress is a statutory requirement**. As a TA you may well be asked to provide information on pupil progress and to attend the pupil review meeting.

Ask the SENCO to set aside some time to talk you through the above. He or she will be able to explain in more detail your school's procedures and practice and then, at a time to suit, you can follow up with further reading.

Behaviour policy

Part 7 of the Education and Inspections Act 2006, Discipline, Behaviour and Exclusion states that:

'The governing body of a relevant school must ensure that policies designed to promote good behaviour and discipline on the part of its pupils are pursued at the school.'….. It further states that it is the head teacher's responsibility 'to determine measures to be taken with a view to: promoting, among pupils, self-discipline and proper regard for authority; encouraging good behaviour and respect for others on the part of pupils and, in particular, preventing all forms of bullying among pupils; securing that the standard of behaviour of pupils is acceptable; securing that pupils complete any tasks reasonably assigned to them in connection with their education; and otherwise regulating the conduct of pupils'.

Although headteachers have final responsibility for writing and implementing their own school policy, putting the policy into practice is the crucial part. For schools to achieve high standards of behaviour there is a real need for consistency amongst all members of staff. You will be expected to follow the guidelines and procedures at all times. It is important that everyone 'sings from the same song sheet'!

Behaviour policy in practice

Most schools provide a practical précis for staff that outlines a progressive procedural process for dealing with behaviour on a day-to-day basis. If your school doesn't have one, ask a member of staff to talk you through the procedures and write your own.

When following the set procedures, these pointers may help you to achieve a positive response from the pupil(s):

- Be calm whilst being firm. If you shout, they may well shout – and more often than not, much louder!
- When asking children to conform to your request for good behaviour always explain why, eg *'I would like you to do this because....'*
- Do not allow the children to negotiate with you – if you do, you allow them to gain control. Say what you would like and stick to it!
- Be consistent. Children will always look for fairness – consistency provides it.

Further advice

Once you're familiar with the three key policies so far discussed, consider going on to look at others. **Remember** – you are part of a whole school team, so:

- **Do** ensure that you have a sound understanding of the school's policies and procedures and that you work within the given guidelines

- **Don't** ignore them. They have a defined purpose and are in place for good reasons

- **Beware** – pupils will ignore rules and guidelines at times. If you are not up to date in your knowledge or if you allow them to negotiate, you will probably let them buck the system

Support for you

Once armed with the basics, there are some other things you will need to know. The table on the next page identifies all the areas you may need information on and the personnel who are most likely to be able to provide it. Usually your line manager will act as a conduit, but if you feel there are gaps in the details and support you have been offered, perhaps use the table to open discussions with your line manager or, where you feel appropriate and confident enough, you may approach the suggested personnel yourself

Information you need

Support/information required	Possible personnel	
A designated job that identifies all defined roles and responsibilities	Headteacher Line manager	Deputy headteacher
Policies, procedures and relevant school, local authority and national guidelines	School secretary Teachers	Line manager Teaching assistants
Information on the pupils	Teachers Pastoral managers	SENCO
Time for planning	Line manager Teachers	
Support in developing appropriate recording and reporting skills	Line manager Teaching assistants	Teachers
Access to wider professional development	Line manager Teacher in charge of professional development	
Appropriate social arrangements	Line manager Teaching assistants	

Flexibility

A common reaction from TAs new to the job is surprise at how flexible and adaptable they need to be. The demands of teachers, pupils and managers are, they say, diverse and wide-ranging. They generally agree, though, that the variety adds to the enjoyment of the job – there's never time to get bored!

Let's start the job!

There are three main areas to a TA's job

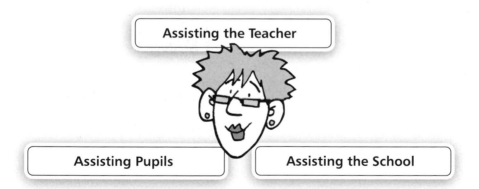

Assisting the Teacher

Assisting Pupils

Assisting the School

The next three chapters look at each area in turn.

The Role of the TA

Assisting the Teacher

Assisting Pupils

Assisting the School

The Profession

Assisting the Teacher

Joint planning – the essentials

Working with teachers is a major part of a TA's work. You need to be clear about what is expected of you, so joint planning with the teacher(s) is really important.

To be successful and to make your job manageable, you need to know:

What do I have to do?

When is it needed?

How am I going to carry it out?

Joint planning – the reality

Not all schools provide adequate opportunities for joint planning, and in secondary schools, where TAs may work with a number of teachers, it may not be realistic. If this is the case in your school, try to ensure that you get, at least, the following:

- Prior knowledge of administrative tasks, with short written instructions
- Copies of lesson plans – you need at least an idea of a lesson's context and content
- Information on pupils with special educational needs. This can be gained from the SENCO. Ask for copies of pupils' Individual Education Plans (IEPs)
- Where specialised individual programmes of work are concerned, it is important that you are given training on how to deliver them so that in these cases you can plan your own work and carry it out successfully.
- Details of how you are expected to record and report requested feedback, if planning/evaluation meetings are not possible

But let's look on the positive side. Many schools do now strive to provide time for teachers and TAs to plan together, so what might that entail?

What to expect

Talking and planning with the teacher will give you a sound understanding of what is expected from you. It should result in more effective support for the teacher and in turn for the pupils' learning.

When joint planning takes place the teacher should talk with you about:

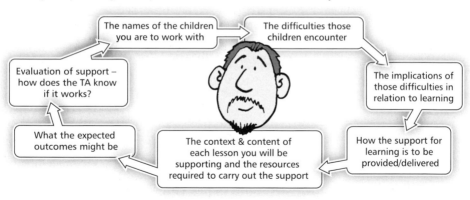

- The names of the children you are to work with
- The difficulties those children encounter
- The implications of those difficulties in relation to learning
- How the support for learning is to be provided/delivered
- The context & content of each lesson you will be supporting and the resources required to carry out the support
- What the expected outcomes might be
- Evaluation of support – how does the TA know if it works?

Identifying tasks

The diagram on page 32 demonstrates how a cycle of planning can help meet pupils' needs. This process should identify a number of tasks that you could undertake to support the teacher in providing for those needs. The work can be split into two categories:

- Working on 'things' ie administrative tasks
- Working with children

Working on 'things' is likely to be the easier of the two, as once explained you can probably carry the tasks out independently.

Working on 'things'

Here are some of the 'things' you might be asked to do and some points to consider before undertaking them.

Looking after resources
Ensuring resources that the teacher identifies are readily available and easily accessible when required

Make sure when the teacher talks about particular resources that you know what they are, where they are kept and when you need to access them.

Photocopying
Reproducing ready-made resources provided by the teacher

Make sure you are shown how to access the photocopier and how to reproduce resources in a range of ways, eg enlarging/reducing, back-to-back copies, multiple copies of pamphlets.

Other tasks, eg:
• Completing dinner registers
• Collecting money
• Supervising pupils at break/lunch times

Make sure you are shown how to complete the tasks you are asked to do and ask if there are any particular rules or regulations you need to abide by.

Working on 'things'

Designing/making resources
Under the direction of the teacher, designing/developing/inventing and producing new resources to support pupils' learning

You may be asked, for example, to make worksheets to a specific design or to develop your own ideas. Make sure the teacher explains exactly what they require and if you are inventing your own, discuss with the teacher both before, during and after the production process.

Looking after the working environment, eg
• Keeping it tidy
• Organising/mounting display work

The teacher may instruct you on what they require or may leave it to you – particularly if you have an artistic bent!

There could be other admin tasks you are asked to do, but whatever the task the main point to remember is to ask for specific instructions. If you don't understand after the initial explanation, ask for further clarification. Don't be afraid – sometimes teachers explain things using jargon and are blissfully unaware that they are doing it!

Working on 'things'

And finally, for your own benefit, you should think about:

Fitting it all in – make sure you plan your time effectively and that the teacher's expectations are realistic. Tasks set should be achievable and within a reasonable time-scale. Trying to fit 10 hours' work into 5 won't work; it will put you under undue pressure, cause stress and set the blood pressure soaring.

Access to the essentials – make sure you're given not just the information but also the resources to carry out a task. Photocopying without paper can prove challenging – particularly if the teacher wants it pronto! Make sure you know where spare paper is kept. If tasks require access to particular resources, talk about this during planning.

Working with children

Now we come to what most TAs say is the best part of the job – working with children. This will probably take up the greatest percentage of your time.

Assisting the teacher in enabling children to understand the work and helping them to achieve to the best of their ability is central to the role of the TA and it's an aspect of their work that teachers value greatly.

The next chapter looks more specifically at methods of assisting pupils and the associated skills; for now we are going to consider the assignments you might be given.

Supporting pupils

Supporting pupils could involve you in one or more of the following:

General in-class support	Small group teaching	Individual Teaching
Supporting all pupils within the lesson, offering help where necessary to enable the pupils to achieve the defined tasks	Supporting • an identified group of pupils with set class work to achieve identified targets • pupils with identified tasks given by the teacher that will have been set at the pupils' level of ability	Working with a pupil • on a designated programme of work aligned to class work • on a specific programme of work aligned to developing particular skills linked to eg literacy, numeracy, behaviour

All three areas will require a sound understanding of the nature of support required. This information may be provided by the teacher or, in cases of pupils with special educational needs, the SENCO. Whoever provides the information, it should direct you towards specific objectives that will enable the pupils to achieve success in learning.

Supporting pupils

Examples of how you might be asked to support pupils:

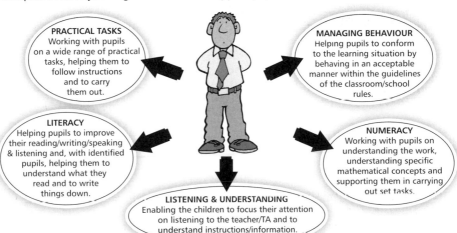

PRACTICAL TASKS
Working with pupils on a wide range of practical tasks, helping them to follow instructions and to carry them out.

MANAGING BEHAVIOUR
Helping pupils to conform to the learning situation by behaving in an acceptable manner within the guidelines of the classroom/school rules.

LITERACY
Helping pupils to improve their reading/writing/speaking & listening and, with identified pupils, helping them to understand what they read and to write things down.

NUMERACY
Working with pupils on understanding the work, understanding specific mathematical concepts and supporting them in carrying out set tasks.

LISTENING & UNDERSTANDING
Enabling the children to focus their attention on listening to the teacher/TA and to understand instructions/information.

Details

Whatever job you are asked to take on, make sure you are provided with appropriate and adequate information on:

- The pupils and their specific needs

- The tasks you are being asked to do and methods/ideas for carrying them out

- The resources you will need

Assessing progress

Part of the job of supporting pupils is helping to assess their progress. This can be invaluable to the teacher, the SENCO and the school. As a TA you are constantly involved with children at close hand. This allows you to build strong relationships and puts you in an excellent position to assess day-to-day progress.

Assessing progress goes hand-in-hand with recording, reporting and evaluating. Although the ultimate responsibility for this belongs to the teacher, the TA is often the one who can provide a lot of the detail in relation to individual pupils. For instance, you will have a lot of opportunity **to observe** pupils and **form an opinion** on their ability to achieve through:

- Watching them while they are working/completing tasks
- Listening to their responses
- Discussing their work with them
- Looking at completed work

This type of assessment is called **formative assessment**.

Formative assessment

In a lesson, formative assessment might involve you observing their ability to:

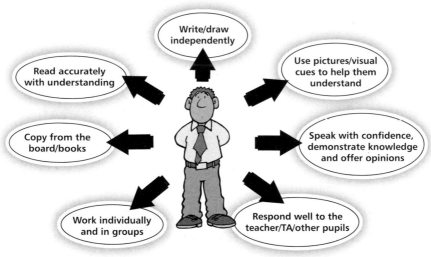

Write/draw independently

Use pictures/visual cues to help them understand

Read accurately with understanding

Copy from the board/books

Speak with confidence, demonstrate knowledge and offer opinions

Work individually and in groups

Respond well to the teacher/TA/other pupils

Formative assessment

After the lesson you may be required to form an opinion by looking at:

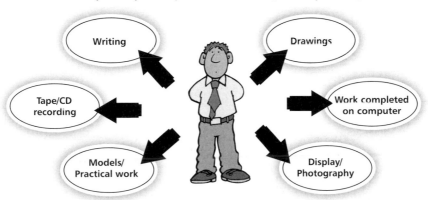

Whether observing before or after class, you are forming an opinion, ie using formative assessment to judge progress. Doing this on a regular basis gives you a very good picture of individuals and groups of pupils and how they are progressing.

Collecting information

You will probably find that you are regularly asked how particular pupils/groups of pupils are getting on. Working closely with them you have more opportunity to notice even the smallest of achievements.

'You are extra eyes and ears for the teacher; you will see things that they sometimes miss, so when they need to assess how particular children are progressing, you will probably be asked for your opinion.'

If you want to do this effectively you will need to ask the teacher:

| What do you want me to assess? | For what purpose? | What are the criteria/measures by which I have to assess progress/achievement? |

Recording information

Once you have established what you are to assess and how, you need to think about how you will record the information. You can use forms or record sheets

- Provided by the teacher
- Designed by yourself
- Aligned to specific standardised assessments

Whichever you use, it should allow for sound accurate recording of information from which you can report back to the teacher verbally or in writing.

When it comes to recording day-to-day progress, lesson planning/record sheets are probably best. They then serve a two-fold purpose: to log information at the planning stage and to record information during/after the lesson. This prevents duplication of paperwork – no need for extra work. Do I hear a cheer? YEAH!

The record sheet

Next question: what should the record sheet look like?
All schools have their own systems of recording and reporting but if you find that your school does not provide TAs with a record/planning sheet, never fear: I have provided an example on the next page.

This record sheet can be used at the planning stage with the teacher to identify:

- Pupils to be supported
- Content of the lesson/work to be covered
- Resources required
- Special considerations, eg the pupil who needs to have work read and explained to her or the one who has the use of an egg timer to help him keep focused for a specific length of time

The rest of the sheet can be completed during or after the lesson to highlight progress, any difficulties that were observed and any action that may need to be taken, eg *'worksheet too difficult for Jasmine to read and understand – adapted ones required for next lesson'*.

The record sheet

Date: ___/___/___

Class to be supported: _____

Name of TA: _____

Lesson/subject: _____

Name of teacher: _____

Support to be offered/ specific groups/pupils to be supported (if any):

Work covered during lesson:

Resources required:

Any special considerations:

Notes:

Action required (if any):

Effective evaluation

Evaluation is about looking at the evidence and forming an opinion on how successful the learning has been. Your record sheet should enable you to do that. It will also allow you to:

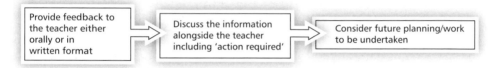

Provide feedback to the teacher either orally or in written format → Discuss the information alongside the teacher including 'action required' → Consider future planning/work to be undertaken

The process of formative assessment relies on judgements made by you and/or the teacher. These are invaluable as you are the person working with the children daily. There are, however, other assessments that take place within schools, known as *summative* and *diagnostic* assessments.

Summative assessment

Perhaps the best examples of summative assessment are tests and exams.
Here children are marked against pre-defined answers/criteria to provide them with a standardised level of attainment.

Exams/tests written by the teacher are used to determine levels of understanding and learning in relation to specific topics/lessons and can assess pupils' progress towards national tests/exams.

National, external exams/tests are used to provide each pupil with a standardised level of attainment. They enable comparisons between children of the same age group within the school, within the Local Authority and countrywide.

When children take part in such assessments there will be very strict guidelines for both the children – eg talking is not permitted – and their teachers to follow. Be mindful of this if you are asked to help supervise such tests/exams.

Summative assessment

Summative assessment is very structured and you could have a vital role to play within it. You could be asked, for example to:

Supervise pupils under exam conditions

Read out instructions/ questions to pupils who have difficulty in reading

Give out/collect in exam or test papers/ equipment

Take dictation from a pupil who has difficulty writing

Mark papers (where the tests and answers have been set by teachers)

Whatever your part, **it is vital to stick to the rules and guidelines**. This is equally important for diagnostic assessments.

Diagnostic assessment

Diagnostic assessment is, as its name implies, used to diagnose difficulties that pupils may be having.

A good example of this type of assessment is a diagnostic reading test. Here a child reads out loud a series of stories that become progressively more difficult. The marking system provides the teacher with a reading accuracy and reading comprehension score, but the test also offers additional information on the processes the child is using to read as observed by the tester.

For example, does the child miss out words, substitute words, guess unknown words, look for pictorial cues? All of these have implications for the child's ability to read and comprehend. Logging their responses will help in planning work to improve their skills.

This is one example of how schools use diagnostic assessment to build profiles of pupils, their levels of ability and their learning needs.

Diagnostic assessment

Information and feedback gained from such diagnostic assessments are invaluable to both teachers and TAs. They provide a much wider understanding of the difficulties a child may be facing in relation to learning and inform the strategies/support that might be used to develop the pupil's skills.

The information is also useful in mapping progress on identified skills to establish how well the pupil is improving. These should be related to specific time-scales, eg the reading test repeated annually will indicate progression over a twelve-month period.

So what might your part in this whole process be?

Diagnostic assessment

As a TA you may be asked to undertake some of the diagnostic assessments, including marking, recording and reporting feedback. If you are to be involved, be sure that you

- Have been adequately trained

- Fully understand the process and are comfortable and confident about running the test before you undertake the process on your own

- Are confident in marking/scoring the test

- Are comfortable with providing feedback to others

- Understand that the regularity of such assessments will vary from test to test and that this will be dictated by the instructions provided – these must be adhered to. (I can still recall the child who had repeated a particular reading test so often that he could recite most of it!)

A working relationship

Having looked at a host of ways in which you may be involved in assisting the teacher, there's one final, but key consideration:

'Getting on with the Teacher'.

This is one of the hardest areas to advise on. Where you get on well with the teacher(s) you are working with then there is no real problem. You are likely to feel confident enough to talk about most things and will have a working relationship that shows mutual respect and is consequently productive and rewarding. The problems arise when this is not the case.

What can you do if your working situation with the teacher is not like this?

The examples on the following pages are real situations that TAs have had to deal with.

Getting on with the teacher

'The teacher doesn't involve me in planning, so when I get to the lesson I don't know what it's about or what I'm expected to do. I just sit amongst the pupils and wait for them to ask for my help.'

The teacher might not even consider that she needs to inform you

Ask politely at the end of the lesson what you are going to be doing next lesson and how they would like you to help.

If this works, as your relationship develops, slowly progress towards asking for longer-term planning and if all goes well, later on ask if you can be involved in the planning.

If no joy, you are unfortunately going to have to 'fly by the seat of your pants' for the time being while you tell your line manager, who should discuss with the teacher.

POINT TO REMEMBER
Many teachers have never been trained to work with TAs. Some find it comes naturally; others find it difficult. With the latter, you are probably going to have to teach them on the job – remember, it's a learning curve for them, so treat them gently!

Getting on with the teacher

'The teacher doesn't like me. It doesn't matter what I do, I always seem to be in the way. She is quite unpleasant to me at times and I feel very intimidated.'

The teacher may be unaware that she is making your life difficult

Find out what the teacher is like with other colleagues/children.

If the teacher treats other colleagues/children well, then it may be that she finds it difficult/threatening to have another adult in the classroom. This is where your personality comes in! Take every opportunity to praise the teacher for the work she is doing so that you take away the threat of being the observer and become the friendly supporter. Once this is established things will definitely improve.

If the teacher treats other colleagues/children in a similar way it's almost certainly not something you're doing wrong. Ask your line manager to look at the situation. They may be able to change your support timetable so that for some of the time you are with other teachers. They should also speak to the teacher concerned, but improvements may be slow.

POINT TO REMEMBER
Even if things are really bad, do not openly talk/gossip about the teacher. Deal with it professionally by discussing it with your line manager or, if you have the confidence, try to talk with the teacher yourself.

Getting on with the teacher

'I'm having difficulty working with my group of children because other pupils in the class are misbehaving and disturbing us. My children are very responsive to my working rules but are obviously having difficulty ignoring the others. The teacher tries but he just shouts at them and they don't listen.'

The teacher may be having difficulty with class discipline

You may need to help both the pupils and the teacher.

Keep working with your group and reinforcing your own rules. Speak calmly and quietly to the other children and try to encourage them to stop disturbing your group by explaining why it is not acceptable. (Children respond better when given reasons rather than demands) This action might help the teacher if he sees the pupils responding to your technique.

Where poor behaviour persists, ask if you can take your group elsewhere to work when possible/appropriate. Talk to your line manager about the discipline difficulties, as they will be able to talk to other colleagues who will be best placed to offer support to the teacher.

POINT TO REMEMBER
Don't openly discuss any teacher's discipline problems with others. This should only be done with identified staff on a professional basis and never in an open forum such as the staffroom.

Getting on with the teacher

The examples given won't cover all the scenarios you may encounter but take time to consider the processes/suggestions, as they could be of use in other situations. They are based on:

- Initial assessment of the situation taking all factors into account – including yourself!

- Looking at the possible options/actions available and deciding which may be best (this can be more than one)

- Making a decision on the actions to be taken and carrying them out

Remember, problems are much easier to sort out if they are shared and discussed.

The Role of the TA

Assisting the Teacher

Assisting Pupils

Assisting the School

The Profession

Assisting Pupils

Working with children

Working with pupils can be the most rewarding and exhilarating experience and is most certainly something to be recommended! There is nothing like observing a pupil and feeling excitement at their achievements, or the feeling of satisfaction in knowing that you have helped them to succeed. All the same, working with children may, at times, be difficult and so a working framework needs to be agreed. This should include establishing

- Mutual respect

- Ground rules for learning and behaviour

- A trusted working relationship

- Understanding among TA, pupils and teacher of the use of accepted systems for withdrawal from lessons

The working framework

Mutual respect
If you give respect you will receive respect. Always lead by example and treat children in the way you would expect to be treated. Children will more often than not respond well to this. Where they aren't respectful, remind them of how they should be responding and **explain why**.

Ground rules
Decide on your rules and regulations for working and discuss them with the pupils, explaining why they are needed. Children need to understand the purpose behind them if they are to conform. Set down your rewards, boundaries and consequences clearly and once they are established don't deviate. (Remember the saying, 'Give an inch and they'll take a mile'? They will!)

The working framework

A working relationship

If you establish mutual respect, a good working relationship will develop. Listening to children and showing empathy and understanding are central to success. Many of the children you work with will have low self-esteem and so lots of praise is needed. Keep telling them they are brilliant – they'll soon warm to you.

Systems for withdrawal

There may be times when supporting a pupil with behavioural difficulties that you need to take them out of the classroom to calm down or settle. This should be a pre-agreed system with the teacher to ensure minimal disruption of the lesson. The system should also be explained to the pupil so they see it as support rather than punishment.

Those who find learning difficult

As a TA working with pupils, a good proportion of your time is likely to be spent with children who have difficulty learning or who have specific needs.

There are several reasons why difficulties arise, eg:

Identified Special Educational Needs

Literacy Weaknesses

Poor Health

Numeracy Weaknesses

HELP!!!

Different Learning Styles

Social Competence

Problems at Home or School

Behaviour

Effects of learning difficulties

Children with learning difficulties might

- Achieve at a slower rate than their peers
- Have difficulty in understanding
- Have difficulty in completing tasks
- Have poor concentration
- Be unable to meet time-scales set down by the teacher

Whatever the difficulty, there is always an impact. Children may

- Become frustrated
- Misbehave
- Be unhappy
- Feel over-tired
- Become disaffected and show total lack of interest in learning/school
- Truant or stop attending

What can TAs do to help?

TAs can offer support in two ways:

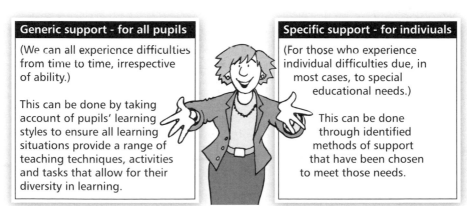

Generic support - for all pupils

(We can all experience difficulties from time to time, irrespective of ability.)

This can be done by taking account of pupils' learning styles to ensure all learning situations provide a range of teaching techniques, activities and tasks that allow for their diversity in learning.

Specific support - for indiviuals

(For those who experience individual difficulties due, in most cases, to special educational needs.)

This can be done through identified methods of support that have been chosen to meet those needs.

Both of these approaches are important. Pages 67 to 72 offer guidance with generic support and pages 81 to 93 with specific support.

Diversity in learning

In order to offer support to pupils in their learning we first of all need to understand how they learn.

In recent years there has been a great deal of research undertaken into how the brain functions and the impact of this upon learning. This has resulted in the wider acceptance that diversity in learning has to be taken into account when teaching and support for learning take place.

We do not all learn in the same way, at the same time or at the same pace – if we did, life would be so much easier. So, what we need to consider is what we can do to help all pupils learn to their maximum potential.

Accelerated learning

Accelerated learning is a term used for an approach to learning that prepares the pupils for learning and provides for different learning styles & needs. Employed effectively, it gives pupils the opportunity to achieve to the best of their ability. Accelerated learning has proved effective for teachers and TAs who have been introduced to the associated techniques & strategies. If you haven't, here goes:

PREPARING THE WAY

Physical state
Children need to be well fed and watered if they are to be able to concentrate and work well. Many schools now provide breakfast clubs, healthy foods at break and lunchtimes and access to water for children at all times. If yours doesn't offer any/all of these, suggest them!

Emotional state
Where children are emotionally upset they will find it extremely difficult to concentrate on learning. Schools which nurture and encourage self-belief are more successful in enabling them to progress. TAs are well placed to offer support, encouragement and praise.

Learning environment
The working environment needs to be the correct temperature, well aired and visually stimulating. Think – how effectively did you learn in a dull, freezing cold classroom? If things aren't right, suggest/offer help in making changes.

The 'big picture'

Once the children are physically and psychologically catered for they are more readily prepared to engage in learning. The way a lesson or session is structured can influence how well pupils learn.

All learners need to be given the 'big picture', ie what they are going to learn and why. We can put the learning into context by

- Explaining/reminding what the topic/learning is about, connecting it to what has gone before and reminding them of long-term goals

- Setting an expectation of learning for the lesson by explaining what is to be learned and what they will be expected to achieve by the end of it

- Telling them what will happen in the following lesson(s) linked to what they are doing this lesson

The lesson starter

Having set the context we are now ready for action!

A starter activity can be used to review prior learning. This is the time to kick-start a lesson with something lively and engaging. It could be, for example, role-play, quick-fire question and answer, an active game to enable them to share their knowledge and understanding. Whatever it is, it should be stimulating enough to 'fire up their interest'.

Now they are ready and willing – what next?

The main part of the lesson and plenary

The main part of the lesson should be a hive of activity. Typically, there will be some input, some active requirement of the pupils and some sharing.

- **Input** – this is where new information is provided and new challenges/goals set. It should involve multi-sensory stimuli, (see following page) eg a dramatised reading, video, role-play, question/answer, etc
- **Activity** – here the pupils engage in a range of activities using their skills to investigate/solve problems/answer questions etc. Their challenges/goals (according to levels of ability) should be re-emphasised
- **Demonstration** – intermittently, the pupils should be asked to share with the class what they have learned/achieved so far

In **the plenary** pupils should be encouraged to review. They should reflect on what has been learned and have the chance to demonstrate their understanding before the teacher or TA informs them 'what happens next'.

To find out more about accelerated learning, see page 125 for recommended books.

Multi-sensory learning

Multi-sensory learning is an approach that will help you to support and teach the pupils you work with. It involves being aware of the way we use our senses to help us to learn. In connection with this, you may hear teachers using the term VAK when they are planning. What does this mean?

 Visual – seeing, having pictures and visual cues

 Auditory – hearing through listening, having auditory stimuli

 Kinaesthetic – touching/feeling/doing by movement and tactile stimuli

VAK

Ideally, pupils should have access to all three ways of learning. Individual learners are not equally strong in all three and so providing visual, auditory and kinaesthetic stimuli gives pupils variety and a number of opportunities to understand and respond.

This can be done through teaching techniques and through pupil tasks. The following lists give some suggestions. Talking with and observing teachers will allow you to see some of these in action.

Visual:
- Pictures
- Diagrams
- Maps
- Mind-maps
- Flow charts
- Use of colour
- Display
- Video

Auditory:
- Speaking
- Radio
- Tapes
- Music
- Use of sound

Kinaesthetic:
- Tactile equipment
- Models
- Practicals
- Role-play
- Games
- Cards
- Brain Gym®

Specific support for those with identified needs

Providing specific support to pupils with identified needs can often be accommodated through the accelerated learning and multi-sensory techniques we have looked at. There will, however, be pupils who require defined support/teaching to enable them to fully engage in the learning process.

As a TA you may be involved with such children and so will need to know:

- The nature of the difficulties
- The support to be offered
- The types of strategies that may be used

This information should be identified on the pupil's Individual Education Plan (IEP) and any TA working with a child with SEN should have access to a copy. You should also be able to gain further information from the SENCO.

Special educational needs

So what special needs might you encounter and what kind of support will be required? To help you here we are going to focus on the following five areas* highlighted in the SEN Code of Practice, looking first at the issues and then (pages 81-89) at strategies for support.

- Communication and interaction
- Cognition and learning
- Sensory and/or physical
- Behaviour/emotional/social
- Medical

Remember, though, some pupils have multi-complex difficulties and will have defined needs in more than one area.

---

* Further research into the difficulties highlighted will provide you with more background. As a start, it's worth visiting the OAASIS website (Office for Advice Assistance Support & Information on Special Needs) at www.oaasis.co.uk . Their information leaflets on a range of SEN provide explanations of named conditions/syndromes, offer ideas on how to provide support, and identify other useful websites.

Communication and interaction

It is important to remember that pupils with speech, language and communication needs are to be found across the whole ability range. Some of these children may have autistic spectrum disorders. These include autism & Asperger's syndrome. Children with speech and language difficulties may have, for example:

- Delayed speech and language skills
- Difficulties with verbal and non-verbal communication
- Difficulty putting things into context
- Poor/little/no abstract thinking
- Poor social skills/interaction
- Poor understanding

- Poor hand-eye co-ordination
- Lack of concentration
- Poor memory
- Poor ordering/organisational skills
- Obsessional tendencies
- Reluctance to change – they like stability

Cognition and learning

Pupils with cognition and learning difficulties may have problems with reading, writing, spelling or manipulating numbers and so will encounter difficulties across the curriculum. Such pupils may be found across the whole ability range and the severity of impairment will vary widely. This category includes pupils with specific learning difficulties such as dyslexia, dyspraxia, dyscalculia and those with moderate and profound learning difficulties. They may struggle with any number of the following:

- Reading accuracy/comprehension
- Spelling
- Writing
- Sequencing
- Concentration/keeping on task
- Organisational skills

- Acquisition of language
- Motor co-ordination
- Manipulating number/mathematical concepts
- Social skills
- Short-term memory

Sensory/physical

Pupils with **sensory difficulties** may have visual impairment, ranging from minor impairment to blindness and/or hearing impairment, ranging from mild hearing loss to being profoundly deaf.

Pupils with **physical difficulties** may be able to access the curriculum and learn without being designated as having SEN. Others, with specific conditions, such as cerebral palsy, heart disease, spina bifida, hydrocephalus, or muscular dystrophy will require specific, identified support.

Visual difficulties cause problems with:	Hearing difficulties cause problems with:	Physical difficulties cause problems with:
Following directions/instructions Seeing the written word in text Seeing/copying from board Co-ordination Writing Understanding	Listening and speaking Understanding/comprehending Co-ordination	Motor skills Access Medical issues

Emotional/social/behaviour difficulties

Pupils with emotional, social and/or behaviour difficulties will have problems learning and will find it hard to conform to school behaviour policies. They may

- Have difficulties with social interaction
- Find it hard to work within established school structures
- Be aggressive towards other children and adults
- Be resistant to accepting responsibility for their behaviour
- Have low self-esteem
- Find it difficult to accept praise

Some of these pupils may have been diagnosed as having specific conditions, such as attention deficit hyperactive disorder (ADHD), Tourette's syndrome, or ASD.

Emotional/social/behaviour difficulties

Such children may display any number of the following:

- Poor social interaction
- Isolation
- Difficulty following instructions
- Temper tantrums
- Difficulty keeping on task
- Difficulty co-operating with adults and children
- Unusual behaviours
- Aggressive behaviour
- Poor memory
- Poor organisational skills
- Poor concentration

Medical

Some pupils may have medical conditions that affect their learning. Their conditions might cause the types of difficulties already highlighted. Illnesses such as epilepsy, asthma, diabetes, can cause disruption to learning through unavoidable absence.

Such children may have conditions that affect their ability to concentrate and which require medication to be administered. Medication may have a calming influence for defined periods.

It is important to note that you should have full understanding or have undergone training before becoming involved in administering medicines.

Having looked at the kinds of SEN you might encounter, let's now focus on support strategies.

Routine and change

All children need **set routines** to help them settle to work more effectively. If they know the expectations and routines and understand the reasons behind them, they have **stability**, **security** and a **feeling of belonging**, especially important for pupils with special needs. In particular, pupils with speech and language difficulties like routine and regularity; they do not cope well with change. Try to pre-empt any changes that you know about, preparing the child by introducing changes gradually. Use visual cues, eg photographs to help them understand what is going to happen.

Or try using **a social story**. Social stories are written around social activities that a child is about to encounter. For example, a social story about changing classrooms and teacher can include the new class, new teacher and details of the new routines. Used alongside regular visits to the new class and teacher, social stories allow for structured, slow progression towards the new situation.

Role-play can be a useful extension to social stories. Visual and active, it is helpful in providing real life situations to reinforce understanding, but be careful to ensure that the pupil is able to cope with it.

Preparing classrooms for pupils

Where pupils with physical difficulties need access to classrooms, or where equipment needs to be set up for pupils with visual impairment, hearing impairment or other learning difficulties, try to get to the classroom ahead of them to get everything ready for the start of the lesson. Remembering what we said about routine, it is important for children to be able to get to their lesson on time and be able to settle straight away, knowing they have everything they need.

Bear in mind, though, the need to discuss with the class teacher. I once received a complaint about a TA who walked into a teacher's lesson before it had ended and began to move some of the children so she could set up a laptop for the next lesson! Be mindful of everyone's needs – including the teacher's.

Instructions

One of the major tasks of a TA is to help children follow instructions.
Some tips:

- Keep the instructions you are giving simple
- Gain eye contact with the child before beginning
- Alert the child, eg *'I am going to.....'* so that they are aware that something is about to happen
- Speak clearly
- Repeat and encourage the child to repeat back and discuss with you to ensure they understand

This process helps all children as it ensures they are focused on the instruction, but it's particularly important for pupils with speech and language difficulties or behaviour, social and emotional difficulties. Where a pupil is still struggling, visual cue cards can be used to show the pupil through pictures/photographs what is required. When you use cue cards, verbalise the action(s) at the same time for reinforcement.

Keeping on task

Going off task is often one of the greatest difficulties that pupils with special needs encounter. They can easily lose concentration and become distracted. They can misbehave due to their particular SEN, or use poor behaviour as a diversionary tactic because they are not able to do the task. Whatever the reason, keeping them on task may well be a real challenge for you. What can you do?

Difficulties with work

Split the work into smaller tasks. Set the first task and tell the pupil what is expected. As they work, encourage the pupil to discuss with you their progress 'so far'. Before moving on to the next small task, ask the pupil to evaluate their own performance/progress, eg *'How do you think that went?' 'Is there anything we could do to improve it?'* This gives you the opportunity to talk and offer support. It also allows you to manipulate the targets as you go along.

Keeping on task

Difficulties with concentrating
Some children are easily distracted. Look at where they are sitting and with whom. Try to find a seating position that has the least number of distractions, eg away from windows and doors and definitely away from pupils who are likely to increase their distraction. Sometimes finding a discreet working space that provides a 'screen' from distractions can work really well, eg an alcove or corner which offers 'protection'.

Difficulties with listening
Some pupils find listening very difficult. You can help to develop active listening skills by devising games, based around their work, that encourage pupils to listen carefully to specific information. Tell them you are going to ask them questions about the information. If you can, let them have the questions in written form as this will help them focus. The key here is to make sure you give the information in manageable 'chunks'. (Sometimes teachers don't and this is when pupils quickly lose interest.)

Keeping on task

Difficulties with behaviour

Where poor behaviour is the issue, establishing ground rules is essential. These should be based around the class/school rules and should focus on what you would like, not what you don't want.

'I would like you to ask permission before moving out of your seat' rather than, *'You are not allowed to move without permission'*.

The latter sets up a challenge for pupils, some of whom will be only too eager to take it on. To support the ground rules, use praise when they comply with requests. Use praise also to encourage them to stay on task. Do take care, however, that your praise is meaningful. No one likes praise if they feel they have not earned it – even pupils with behaviour difficulties.

Use rewards to support your praise and their achievements.

Be firm

Where a pupil continues to ignore requests to comply with instructions, and the offer of a reward is not working, use choice and consequence: *'Darren, you can either choose to sit down or you will be choosing to stay behind for five minutes.'* Use classroom/school sanctions here so that the pupil is dealt with in exactly the same way as other children.

Ignore this at your peril – children are really 'hot' on things being fair.

Where you have developed a good working relationship with a pupil you can often use discreet signals to encourage particular responses, eg finger to lips to be quiet; using the basketball time-out to tell them to move to a special place where they can calm down. As you work with pupils you will devise your own that are just as effective.

Reading and scribing

Some pupils may not be able to actively participate in the lesson when individual reading and writing are required and you might be asked to read and write for them. Do be careful here: what you write should be the child's thoughts and not your own ideas or interpretation. You must also take care when you are asked to read and write for a pupil during an external test/exam, eg SATs or GCSEs. If you falter because you know an answer they give you is wrong, they will pick it up. I know from experience:

'It's wrong isn't it Miss?'
'No, no, I was just trying to get myself comfortable in the chair!'
'No, I know it's wrong – should it be....' And so it went on.

What alerted them? My body language and my hesitation in writing it down. So, be mindful of this. It's a difficult skill to master but practising during internal tests will help.

Differentiating worksheets

Simplifying a worksheet created by the teacher gets easier with experience. You'll find when you first start supporting pupils you are automatically simplifying by explaining. Over time, you will become more aware of what your pupils can and cannot understand. You can then adapt worksheets and, indeed, design your own. For example, where teachers are using heavily text-based sheets, simplify the language and find pictures to include for visual cues.

For pupils with visual impairments, you may need to enlarge text, either on the computer or on a photocopier.

Delivering individual programmes of work

You might be asked to deliver specific programmes of work, for example, a literacy programme based on multi-sensory teaching or a numeracy programme requiring work on a specific concept. This type of work needs to be very precise, so ideally it should be planned with the SENCO or teacher.

Appropriate training and guidance will help you to deliver the programmes successfully and – just as importantly – with confidence.

The same is true when you support pupils in their use of ICT (information communication technology). A short time spent familiarising yourself with the programmes or equipment will give you confidence. Make sure your line manager knows what training you need.

Using ICT

Some areas in which you might be asked to support pupils using ICT:

- Word processing or using other software to help with writing tasks or with developing reading and writing skills

- After using tape recorders with pupils who find it difficult to 'tell their stories' in writing, you might then help them to transcribe on computer afterwards

- Finding resources to use with pupils with specific needs, eg software that enhances interactive communication through pictures and sound

- Using specific software that allows pupils with both sensory and physical difficulties to read, write and produce work

- Working alongside pupils with behavioural difficulties who have been given access to computers as a reward. Specific rules should be agreed with the teacher and pupil in advance

Supporting pupils outside the classroom

You might be needed to escort pupils from room to room or to observe them closely at breaks or lunchtimes where confrontation with others might occur. Using this time to chat to them will help you build up a good relationship that will be mutually beneficial. As pupils get to know you, you will find that whenever they need help, they will come looking for you. You can help them to develop their own skills, eg in managing their own behaviour. Try taking them through this process:

- What happened?
- Why do you think it happened?
- What were the consequences?
- Do you think it was fair?
- Why/why not?
- What do you think we could do about it? What might you do differently next time?

This process will help you to help the child reflect on what has happened and help them to make valued decisions/choices based on fairness and respect.
This process should be used both in and out of lessons.

Physical/first-aid/medical support

You might be asked to

- Use specialist equipment to support pupils with physical difficulties
- Issue/administer particular medication to identified pupils
- Take care of pupils who need dressing/toileting/support for personal issues

In each of these instances, make sure you receive appropriate training and that you are familiar with school guidelines.

Further your knowledge

This section has offered an introduction to some of the ways you might be required to support pupils. The diagram below suggests ways you might further your knowledge.

Seeking additional advice/help from:

- Teachers
- SENCO
- Support agencies
- Voluntary organisations
- Other TAs
- Research

Sharing good practice by:

- Observing teachers/ other TAs
- Exchanging successful strategies / ideas
- Looking at websites that offer good-practice exemplars

Whatever support you offer will help the children you are working with, and seeing them progress and achieve is extremely rewarding.

The Role
of the TA

 Assisting
the Teacher

 Assisting
Pupils

 Assisting the
School ◀

 The Profession

Assisting
the School

School-wide support

Having looked at supporting teachers and pupils, the following pages explain the kind of support you might be expected to offer the whole school. There are three key areas:

- Curriculum support
- Extra curricular activities
- Additional duties

Curriculum support

As well as assisting the teacher in planning and delivering the defined curriculum, TAs might also be assigned whole-school responsibilities to help with **ICT, literacy and numeracy** through:

- Joint planning for support across the curriculum
- Delivery of specified programmes of work
- Development of resources/support materials
- Evaluating/recording/reporting progress

You need to be aware of who you report back to when completing set tasks: a subject teacher, curriculum leader or senior manager?

Extra curricular activities

All schools offer a range of extra curricular activities. They provide a means of further developing pupils' personalities, practical and social skills, giving them opportunities to experience a range of physical and mental challenges and to discover hidden talents.

Activities or clubs may run before school, during lunchtimes or after school. You might like to volunteer to support some of them. This gives you the chance to work with and observe pupils in a different learning environment and so develop your understanding of their personalities and interests beyond the classroom. It also lets the pupils see you in a different context and can have a positive effect on your working relationships.

Where schools specifically ask TAs to cover clubs or activities as part of their defined role, it ought to be as an accepted part of their working hours and be defined in the contract of employment.

Additional duties

As a TA you may be asked to do a number of jobs to support the school in its efficient and effective running. Your contract of employment should identify these, eg

- Taking care of/issuing/administering prescribed **medicines**. Ensure that you are fully trained in line with policy and procedure

- Working as a **trained 'first-aider'.** You may be asked to undertake training and have some responsibility for administering first-aid within the school

- **Playground/break duty**. This may be a general duty or could involve supporting identified pupils. Whichever, you will need direction on what is expected, what the duty entails and a copy of the school's policies covering such responsibilities

- **Collecting money**. This needs careful administration to ensure all monies are accounted for. Schools will have set procedures/practices. Whatever the system, when you hand over money, always ensure someone signs for it

And there's more...

- Completing **attendance registers**. The morning and afternoon attendance register is a legal document; if you are asked to take it, make sure you mark it accurately. Class registers are not legal documents, but nonetheless, be vigilant if you are asked to record details of absence

- As a TA you might have to help in escorting pupils to and from a **swimming pool**. If you have appropriate qualifications, you could be asked to teach swimming. As always, be sure you know and follow school policies, guidelines and procedures

Whatever duties you undertake as a TA, for your own protection have regard not only to the school's policies, procedures and practice, but to LA directives and national guidelines, particularly where legislation/law is an issue.

The Role
of the TA

 Assisting
the Teacher

 Assisting
Pupils

 Assisting the
School

 The Profession ◀

The Profession

National Workload Agreement

The role of the teaching assistant has changed over the years, with designated roles and responsibilities becoming more defined. The National Workload Agreement identified tasks teachers should no longer be responsible for:

- Collecting money
- Chasing absences
- Bulk photocopying
- Copy typing
- Producing standard letters
- Producing class lists
- Record keeping & filing
- Classroom display
- Analysing attendance figures
- Processing exam results
- Collating pupil reports
- Administering work experience
- Administering examinations
- ICT trouble-shooting and minor repairs
- Ordering supplies and equipment
- Commissioning new ICT equipment
- Stocktaking
- Cataloguing
- Minuting meetings
- Co-ordinating and submitting bids
- Seeking and giving personnel advice
- Managing pupil data
- Inputting pupil data

National Workload Agreement

In addition

- Teachers will not routinely be asked to invigilate external exams
- The amount of cover they provide for absent colleagues has been reduced
- Time has been set aside for planning, preparation and assessment work

Schools therefore need other personnel to carry out such duties. In the light of this, frameworks have been developed in local areas to outline the professional structure for support staff and teaching assistants. These frameworks should include guidance on pay structure, job profiles and associated qualifications. They may also provide advice to schools on how to recruit, retain and develop their teaching assistants.

As a TA you need to be aware that there is no overarching national template for such frameworks; local areas are responsible for developing their own. Your school or education authority can provide you with a copy of the framework in your local area.

What's in a local framework?

Your local framework should offer you information on:

Grading Structure

Providing you with a pay spine to determine the grading of TAs in line with the associated job profiles

Job Profiles

Giving you an identifiable grade level aligned to the defined pay structure and providing you with an outline or description of what is expected from you in the job. It should also state specific requirements in relation to experience, qualifications and knowledge/skills

Career Development

Through job profiles there should be an evident structure for career progression with identifiable increased levels of responsibility and autonomy

Training

Identifying routes to training that will support the development of your skills, providing opportunities for career development

Job profiles

Job profiles should identify the level at which a job is set and the associated pay scale. They should also provide you with a job description identifying what you will be expected to do if you take up the post:

Level:
This should state the level of responsibility assigned to the job from 1 – 4, with 4 being Higher Level Teaching Assistant.

It may also give an overview of:
• Who the TA is responsible to
• The range of work to be undertaken

Support for:
Will identify, within the school, who the TA is to support and the range of tasks that may be expected in assisting:

• Pupils
• Curriculum
• Teacher(s)
• School

To see what a job profile might look like, follow the instructions on the next page.

Job profiles

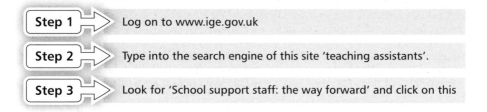

Step 1 → Log on to www.ige.gov.uk

Step 2 → Type into the search engine of this site 'teaching assistants'.

Step 3 → Look for 'School support staff: the way forward' and click on this

You might like to print a copy of the above document as it will prove useful in relation to the section in this book on career progression and training (pages 109-111).

Higher level teaching assistants

With the inception of the Workforce Agreement and its recognition of the significant contribution support staff make to the successful functioning of schools came the new role, 'higher level teaching assistant' (HLTA).

This brought with it the need to identify the skills and attributes required by HLTAs for carrying out their role. Although schools had always identified the roles and responsibilities of their TAs, they had never had to identify them at this level.

In line with this, the Teacher Training Agency (TTA) developed agreed national professional standards by which to measure competencies to take account of the fact that HLTAS undertake a more extended role in supporting the work of schools and their teachers. Schools now have the opportunity to use these standards to assess TAs who wish to progress to HLTA status.

HLTA professional standards

More detailed information on the standards can be obtained from the TTA website **www.tta.gov.uk** where you can access information by typing **HLTA** into the search box. When this takes you to the next page, look for **'go to key publications'**. Here you will find the following documents available to download:

* *'Professional standards for higher level teaching assistant'*

* *'Guide to the standards – meeting the professional standards for the award of higher level teaching assistant status'*

* *'Handbook for candidates – meeting the professional standards'*

These will give you a good picture of what the role of the HLTA is all about.

Whatever level you are currently working at, you can aspire to the level of HLTA.

Career progression and training

Career progression is available for all teaching assistants provided competencies and expertise can be demonstrated through qualifications, training and/or employer references.

Whether you are applying for a job as a TA or are currently working within a school, you should be made aware of the opportunities for **C**ontinued **P**rofessional **D**evelopment (CPD). This is something that both schools and Local Authorities should be offering in their role as employers.

CPD provides schools with well-informed, skilled personnel who are more able to carry out their designated work and, as a teaching assistant, CPD is just as important for you as it is for the teaching staff.

CPD

CPD enables you to perform your role with more confidence and increased competence. So, what sort of training is available?

Generic/whole school

Training that focuses on issues relevant to school development/ improvement and locally identified issues

Individual

- Specific training in relation to working with pupils, eg behaviour management, child protection

Or

- Training related to achievement of Vocational Qualifications or Professional Standards in relation to your job as a TA

Generic/whole school training

Your school ought to involve you in its in-service training (INSET) wherever it is relevant to you. This type of training may take place on days when the pupils are not in school or during 'twilight' sessions, ie after school. If you are not invited to participate and think that you should be, talk to your line manager about it.

Much of the training you gain as a TA is 'picked up' incidentally by observing teachers or other colleagues working with and managing pupils. Take time to notice how children respond to different adults, to their working environment and to other pupils. Learn from both the good and bad practice you see.

By sharing your observations and knowledge, you can possibly become the 'trainer'. The next page gives an excellent example of this. It's from a TA during a training session where groups of TAs were exchanging ideas.

Thomas the 'twitcher'

'Thomas, a year 7 boy, was having difficulty in some lessons because he couldn't sit still. He was always moving, fidgeting, tapping the table with his pen, twitching his legs under the desk, etc. I noticed he often came into conflict with teachers who insisted he 'sit still and stop fidgeting' and was regularly sent out of the lesson. However, with one particular teacher Thomas was always responsive and well behaved. That teacher was very aware when Thomas became restless and at these times would give him the opportunity to move. He might give him a job to do like handing out equipment or, when asking him to respond to questions, he'd encourage Thomas to stand and, if he wished, move around while talking. These and other strategies seemed to work very well, so I decided to discuss them with the teacher.

The teacher explained that Thomas had told him he found it difficult to stay still for any length of time. When he was asked to do so, he often became very agitated inside; he felt he had to move or he would explode. That's when the teacher started looking for strategies to help Thomas cope.

I suggested the teacher tell other staff about his solution, but he was reluctant and not sure how to set about doing it. That's when I got the idea...

The TA's response

She went on to explain that she suggested to her line manager a monthly 'HELP' magazine for the staffroom which could be used to inform staff about ideas, strategies or information they had on particular pupils or groups of pupils. It could include what worked with pupils and highlight what caused difficulties. The TA offered to collate the information and it was agreed that the SENCO should see the items prior to printing and distribution.

She said the process had been in place for about six months and was proving to be popular with most members of staff, though we all agreed at this point that 'you can't please all of the people all of the time' – especially true in schools!

This is just one example of a TA sharing information and helping others. The great bonus was that it was achieved in a non-threatening way. Great idea – why not give it a go?

Individual training

When considering the type of training you might undertake as an individual, ask yourself the following questions:

1. What is the purpose of the training?_____
   _____

2. Who will it benefit?   Me ☐   Pupils ☐   Other colleagues ☐   School ☐

3. Will it provide a higher level of expertise within the school?   YES/NO
   If yes, how? _____

4. Will it help me to enhance my own skills/career?   YES/NO
   If, yes, how? _____

The benefits

Having asked yourself the questions, you can determine whether the identified training will prove valuable. You can also demonstrate to your school that you are able to make well-informed decisions relating to the support you will be able to offer and to your own career development.

Answering the questions may also be useful if you are requesting funding for training. Schools and LAs have allocated monies for CPD and, if you were to request financial support they may well ask for the reasoning and predicted outcomes/benefits.

As a professional, you should strive to access training at every given opportunity. Enhancing your skills through CPD will benefit you and those who work with you.

Finding opportunities

There are numerous training providers/organisations and, ideally, your school or LA will recommend and offer courses. The following websites, though, provide some starting points.

www.teachernet.gov.uk/teachingassistants – information on TA training and qualifications, including DfES Induction Training & National Occupational Standards

www.hlta.gov.uk – information on HLTA training and assessment

www.tda.gov.uk/support.aspx – information on National Vocational Qualifications and National Occupational Standards

www.qca.org.uk – information on National Qualifications Framework and National Vocational Qualifications

Take your time considering what's on offer and talk to people who have already undergone training to help you make an informed decision. You will then need to make your training requests to your line manager or LA, giving details including costs and training provider.

Evaluating and recording

Keep a record of your continued professional development including the range of skills/expertise you have acquired and the impact the training has had.

- What was the training?

- To what extent did it increase your knowledge, confidence and competence?

- The outcomes post-training – was it worthwhile? Has it had impact? Have you used and shared the expertise that you gained?

Accessing support

There will be times when you require support, whether to carry out your job effectively or to overcome a difficulty that has personal implications. The internet may answer some of your queries. The best website is **www.teachernet.gov.uk** which provides a wealth of information relating to schools and education and has a specific area for TAs.

The following diagrams, meanwhile, show you where to find information and support in school.

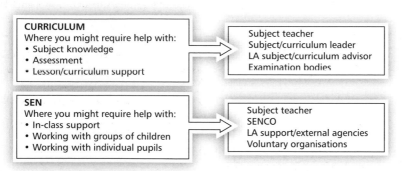

CURRICULUM
Where you might require help with:
- Subject knowledge
- Assessment
- Lesson/curriculum support

Subject teacher
Subject/curriculum leader
LA subject/curriculum advisor
Examination bodies

SEN
Where you might require help with:
- In-class support
- Working with groups of children
- Working with individual pupils

Subject teacher
SENCO
LA support/external agencies
Voluntary organisations

Accessing support

PASTORAL SUPPORT
Where you might need help with:
• Supporting pupils with personal problems
• Dealing with child protection issues

→

Classroom teacher/form tutor
Head of year/key stage manager
Pastoral manager
SENCO
School's child protection officer

HEALTH & SAFETY
Where you might need help with:
• Unsafe working environment
• Faulty equipment
• Risk assessments for working with pupils
• Risk assessments regarding school trips

→

Site manager/caretaker
Your line manager
Member of the school's senior management team
School's health and safety officer
School/local union representative

PERSONAL ISSUES
Where you might need help because of
difficulties with:
• Pupils
• Other staff
• Parents

→

Teaching staff
Pastoral staff
Line manager
Member of the school's senior management team
School/local union representative

Whatever issue you are facing, there is always help at hand. School handbooks often identify routes for support alongside named personnel.

Professional associations

If you encounter a difficult situation where in-school support is insufficient, then you can always turn to your professional association. If you are not already a member of a union, consider joining one. Professional associations are primarily there to protect your interests. Investigate those which enrol TAs and talk to other colleagues and members before making a decision on which one is likely to be the best for you in your working situation.

Handling conflict

As part of a profession that has a major impact on our children, you are in a position to build relationships and trust with them and they will sometimes rely heavily on you. Their need is often far reaching and some pupils will certainly view you as their trusted friend.

This relationship is very different from the one you will have with teachers and occasionally you may find yourself in difficulty where there is conflict between pupil and teacher. Many TAs find this situation stressful. Who to support? Teacher or pupil?

Handling conflict

There isn't an easy answer to these questions but as a professional you need to make an informed choice. How would you feel if you were the teacher? How would you feel if you were the pupil? From those positions you can judge how best to respond.

Children respect honesty and integrity and have a great sense of fairness. Most of the time they will accept the decisions made. You can help them by talking through situations. Discuss the appropriateness of their actions and responses, your actions and responses and the teacher's actions and responses.

Keep smiling!

To be a true professional you should assess, evaluate and adapt your practice according to need. At the start of the book you were asked to consider evaluating your practice in the light of what you were about to read. I hope this book has helped you to do that.

Working with children can be very stressful but there are many times when they make us smile and lift our spirits. I would like to leave you with a couple of examples on the next page of what I call the' laughter tonic'. They are taken from the book A *Pis of Cak* by Peter A. Jeffcock which gives examples of children's writing. Read, smile and stay happy!

The laughter tonic

'The total is when you add up all the numbers and a remainder is an animal that pulls Santa's sleigh'.*

'The lady who stoped peple from being nasty to black peple was Rachel Ickwality'.*

* Taken from *A Pis of Cak* by Peter A. Jeffcock

Further information: books

A Lot to Say: A guide for social workers, personal advisers and others working with disabled children and young people with communication impairments
by Jenny Morris
Published by Scope, 2002

A Pis of Cak by Peter A Jeffcock
Published by Summersdale Publishers Ltd, 2000

Accelerated Learning: A User's Guide by Alistair Smith, Mark Lovatt, Derek Wise
Published by Network Educational Press, 2003

Accelerated Learning Pocketbook by Brin Best
Published by Teachers' Pocketbooks, 2004

Behaviour Management Pocketbook by Peter Hook & Andy Vass
Published by Teachers' Pocketbooks, 2004

The Brain's Behind It by Alistair Smith
Published by Network Educational Press, 2002

Children First: A Guide to Needs of Disabled Children in School
RADAR (The Royal Association for Disability & Rehabilitation
Published by Lamport Gilbert Limited, 1997

Further information: books

Inclusion Pocketbook by Niki Elliot, Elaine Doxey & Val Stephenson
Published by Teachers' Pocketbooks, 2004

Introducing Children to Mind Mapping by Eva Hoffman
Published by Learn to Learn, 2001

Learning to Learn by Gary Burnett
Published by Crown House Publishing, 2002

Removing Barriers to Achievement: The Government's Strategy for SEN
DfES, 2004

Writing Frames by Birmingham Advisory & Support Services
Published by BASS, 2001

And the following, published by Edu-Kinesthetics Inc.

Brain Gym®
P. Dennison & G. Dennison

Brain Gym® Teacher's Edition
P. Dennison & G. Dennison

The Learning Gym
E. Ballinger

Edu-K for Kids
P. Dennison & G. Dennison

Brain Gym® Surfer
S. Hinsley

About the author

Dot Constable

Dot Constable is a former deputy headteacher and SENCO with over 25 years' experience working in the education system. Having worked in schools in challenging circumstances, she has developed expertise in improving the quality of teaching and learning, in providing appropriate support for pupils with special educational needs and in improving classroom management and pupil behaviour. Now working as an education consultant she provides support, guidance and training to schools, LEAs and teaching agencies. Her greatest goal is to have a positive impact on the educational provision children encounter to enable them to have that 'feel good factor' about their learning experiences.

Dot would be happy to help you to initiate or develop ideas provided within this book or to offer further help, support and guidance. She can be contacted directly by email at dconstable@wv15.freeserve.co.uk

Order Form

Your details

Name _____

Position _____

School _____

Address _____

_____

_____

Telephone _____

Fax _____

E-mail _____

VAT No. (EC only) _____

Your Order Ref _____

Please send me:

		No. copies
Teaching Assistant's _____	Pocketbook	☐
_____	Pocketbook	☐
_____	Pocketbook	☐
_____	Pocketbook	☐
_____	Pocketbook	☐

Order by Post

**Teachers'
Pocketbooks**

Laurel House, Station Approach
Alresford, Hants. SO24 9JH UK

Order by Phone, Fax or Internet

Telephone: +44 (0)1962 735573
Facsimile: +44 (0)1962 733637
E-mail: sales@teacherspocketbooks.co.uk
Web: www.teacherspocketbooks.co.uk